Animals in the Wild

Crocodile and Alligator

by Vincent Serventy

ISBN 0-590-44722-X

 This edition published by Scholastic Inc., 730 Broadway, New York, NY 10003, by arrangement with John Ferguson Pty Ltd.

12 11 10 9 8 7 6 5 4 3 2 3 4 5/9

Printed in the U.S.A.

SCHOLASTIC INC.
New York Toronto London Auckland Sydney

Alligators and crocodiles were on earth 200 million years ago. These reptiles and their relatives, the dinosaurs, were the strongest animals of their time.

Alligators are found in North and South America and in China. Crocodiles live in most tropical countries. This is a Nile crocodile from Africa.

This saltwater crocodile's teeth can be seen clearly even when its mouth is closed. The large fourth tooth in its lower jaw fits into a groove on the outside of the upper jaw.

An alligator's mouth is different. When it is closed, the large fourth tooth cannot be seen. It fits into a pit in the upper jaw. Alligators, such as this American alligator, have larger noses and snouts than crocodiles.

The nostrils and eyes are the only parts above water when this Australian freshwater crocodile wants to look around without being seen.

Although they can stay underwater for long periods all crocodiles and alligators must come to the surface to breathe. Their back feet are webbed between the claws and this helps them tread water. They swim by beating their powerful tails.

When on land a crocodile usually lies on its stomach, or moves along slowly, with its body close to the ground. If in a hurry it lifts its body higher and can move at a speed of 12 miles an hour.

Like all reptiles, crocodiles and alligators are cold-blooded. On cold days or during strong winds they lie in the water to keep themselves warm. On hot days they come out to sunbathe.

This caiman crocodile lives in the rivers of South and Central America. It has a very tough skin. Even when it is hurled against rocks in the river rapids this strong armor protects the caiman from damage.

Not a floating log, but a floating crocodile, this salt-water crocodile from northern Australia waits in the river for a victim. Animals coming to drink at the river bank may realize their danger too late.

Even out of the water some animals are not safe from crocodiles and alligators.

This American alligator is trying to catch a baby egret which has climbed as high as it can to escape.

This hungry swamp crocodile from Sri Lanka is devouring the carcass of a python it has killed.

When the victim is a large animal, several crocodiles will often fight over the carcass.

The saltwater crocodile can grow over eleven feet long and weigh more than a ton. It catches most of its prey in the water and eats a lot of fish and crabs. It also scavenges for food along river banks.

The Nile crocodile's main food is fish and other water creatures, but it will attack larger animals. With one swing from its powerful tail, it can knock a cow or an antelopc into the water.

The saltwater crocodile builds her nest out of leaves and soil. The mother lays up to fifty eggs and often stays nearby to protect them. After three months in the warm soil the babies chip their way out of the eggs.

The Nile crocodile builds a nest in river sandbanks. When the babies are ready to hatch they call out to their mother from inside the eggs. She digs out the mound to help them get out.

When her babies are out of the nest the Nile crocodile gathers them all up in her mouth.

With her whole family safe in her "carrying bag" she heads off to the water and releases them there!

The eggs and babies have many enemies. Large lizards and wild pigs dig up the nests and eat the eggs. Buffaloes accidentally trample the nests. Sea eagles can catch baby crocodiles in their sharp talons.

Safe for the moment, a baby crocodile rests near the water's edge. Once fully grown, its only enemy is man. In many parts of the world crocodiles and alligators are hunted for their beautiful skins.

Acknowledgements are due to Vincent Serventy for all photographs in this book except the following:
Bruce Coleman Ltd, Giuliano Capelli p 2–3; G. L. Bernard p 10; Bruce Coleman Ltd, Donn Renn p 12–13; Bruce Coleman Ltd, Dieter and Mary Plage p 14, 15; Oxford Scientific Films, Maurice Tibbles p 17; Oxford Scientific Films, David Curl p 18, 23; Bruce Coleman Ltd, Jen and Des Bartlett p 19; Bruce Coleman Ltd, John Visser p 20; Natal Parks Board p 21.